Chemical Disinfection in Hospitals

GAJ Ayliffe
D Coates
PN Hoffman

Public Health Laboratory Service

CHEMICAL DISINFECTION IN HOSPITALS

© Public Health Laboratory Service 1984, 1993

First published 1984
Second edition 1993

Published by the Public Health
Laboratory Service
61 Colindale Avenue
London NW9 5DF

ISBN 0 901144 34 7

Printed by The Blackmore Press, Shaftesbury

Chemical Disinfection in Hospitals

CONTENTS

PRINCIPLES OF
CHEMICAL DISINFECTION

Definitions

In order to define the role of chemical disinfection it is necessary to distinguish between sterilisation and disinfection. For the purposes of this book the following definitions apply.

sterilisation. A process used to render an object free from all living organisms.

disinfection. A process used to *reduce* the number of micro-organisms but not usually of bacterial spores; the process does not necessarily kill or remove all micro-organisms, but reduces their number to a level which is not harmful to health. The term is applicable to the treatment of inanimate objects and materials and may also be applied to the treatment of the skin, mucous membranes and other body tissues and cavities.

cleaning. A process that removes contaminants including dust, soil, large numbers of micro-organisms and the organic matter (e.g. faeces, blood) that protects them. Cleaning is an always useful, sometimes essential, prerequisite to disinfection and sterilisation.

decontamination. A general term for the destruction or removal of microbial contamination to render an item safe. This will include methods of cleaning, disinfection and sterilisation.

chemical disinfectant. A compound that can destroy vegetative organisms and most viruses. The term 'antiseptic' is used for non-toxic disinfectants which are applied to the skin or living tissues. A **sterilant** is a chemical disinfectant which can, under certain stringent conditions, destroy bacterial spores, viruses and vegetative organisms. This form of sterilisation does not have the same degree of sterility assurance as that achieved by physical methods, e.g. steam sterilisation.

Sterilisation

Sterilisation can be achieved by physical methods, such as heating in an autoclave (moist heat) or hot-air oven (dry heat), and low-temperature steam and formaldehyde, ionising irradiation, membrane filtration, or chemical methods (e.g. ethylene oxide gas). Of these methods, only autoclaving is both simple to perform and widely applicable in hospitals, but is unsuitable for thermolabile items such as flexible fibre-optic endoscopes and many plastic devices. Methods of sterilisation have been standardised for most purposes and the growth of sterile services departments (SSDs) and the manufacture of sterile single-use products have lessened the burden upon medical and nursing staff of organising and supervising their own sterilisation procedures.

Disinfection

Disinfection is best achieved by moist heat such as boiling, which kills all organisms except some bacterial spores and 'slow viruses', even in the presence of organic matter. Steam at subatmospheric pressure and pasteurisation at temperatures between 65°C and 80°C are also highly effective against vegetative bacteria and viruses. A combination of cleaning and thermal disinfection is commonly used for dirty instruments returned to SSDs, bedpan washer–disinfectors, laundry and dishwashers.

Chemical disinfection

Chemical disinfection is inherently complicated because of the number and variety of factors that influence the antimicrobial activity of disinfectants: micro-organisms vary in their sensitivity to different disinfectants. Gram-positive bacterial species are usually sensitive, Gram-negative species less sensitive, tubercle bacilli relatively resistant, and bacterial spores extremely resistant. Viruses also vary in their response to disinfectants, depending on their structure. Enveloped (lipid-containing) viruses are killed by most disinfectants but non-enveloped viruses tend to be more resistant.

Most disinfectants are effective against a limited range of micro-organisms, and very few are usefully sporicidal. Wherever possible, disinfectants should only be used on clean surfaces as they may fail to penetrate overlying soil such as blood or pus on instruments, and faecal residues on bedpans. Furthermore, they may be inactivated by organic matter, detergents with which they are incompatible, hard water and materials such as cork, rubber and plastic.

Many disinfectants are unstable and, after chemical breakdown has occurred, the solution may have little or no antimicrobial activity and may support the growth and proliferation of such versatile organisms as the pseudomonads. Hence it is essential that fresh dilutions of disinfectant are made up regularly in clean, preferably heat-treated, containers. Many disinfectants are also corrosive and irritant, and protective clothing and disposable gloves must be worn when handling them. In addition, items immersed in disinfectants usually require thorough rinsing before use and this can lead to recontamination.

The antimicrobial activity of disinfectants can be dependent upon pH; for example, glutaraldehyde has greater antimicrobial activity in alkaline conditions. However, the more active state of a compound may be less stable, such as in hypochlorites for example, which are supplied at high pH and glutaraldehyde which is supplied at low pH. The compounds can be buffered to the most appropriate pH immediately before use, but will then be usable for only a limited period.

Disinfectants vary markedly in the rate at which they kill micro-organisms. Chlorine-based agents and alcohols act quickly, killing vegetative bacteria in as little as 1–2 min on clean surfaces, whereas some other disinfectants may take hours. Some disinfectants may just inhibit the growth of bacteria rather than kill them, i.e. they are bacteriostatic rather than bactericidal. Quaternary ammonium compounds, for example, are mainly bacteriostatic at very low concentrations, whereas at high concentrations they are bactericidal. Consequently, the effectiveness of chemical disinfection is often uncertain and, wherever possible, disinfection by heat is preferable to use of chemical methods.

Efficient cleaning removes a high proportion of any micro-organisms present, including bacterial spores, and in many hospital situations, thorough cleaning of the environment or items of equipment is adequate. For example, domestic cleaning of hospital floors and walls is generally sufficient, and additional chemical disinfection is wasteful. Similarly, in wards, cleaning of locker-tops, furniture, ledges and shelves is adequate, unless the surfaces are contaminated with potentially infectious material such as blood, faeces, pus or sputum. Anionic and non-ionic detergents have a good detergent activity and are usually used for environmental cleaning. Cationic detergents (e.g. quaternary ammonium compounds) show some antimicrobial activity but are usually less efficient detergents.

Risk categories and decontamination

The choice of method of disinfection or sterilisation depends on a number of factors, which include the type of material to be treated, the organisms involved, the time available for decontamination, and the risks to staff and patients. The risks to patients from equipment and the environment may be classified as detailed on the page opposite.

High risk	Definition	Items in close contact with a break in skin or mucous membrane or introduced into a normally sterile body area
	Examples	Surgical instruments, syringes, needles, intrauterine devices and associated equipment, dressings, urinary and other catheters
	Suitable method	Sterilisation required. Disinfection which includes *M. tuberculosis* but not necessarily atypical mycobacteria or spores may sometimes be acceptable if sterilisation is not possible or practicable
Intermediate risk	Definition	Items in contact with mucous membranes or other items contaminated with particularly virulent or readily transmissible organisms; or items to be used on highly susceptible patients
	Examples	Respiratory equipment, gastroscopes
	Suitable method	Disinfection required, by heat where possible
Low risk	Definition	Items in contact with normal and intact skin
	Examples	Stethoscopes, washing bowls
	Suitable method	Cleaning and drying usually adequate

Items not in close contact with patients or their immediate surroundings, e.g. floors, walls, ceiling, sinks and drains, present a minimal risk to patients.

PROPERTIES OF CHEMICAL DISINFECTANTS

The general properties of important groups of disinfectants are given below. These properties may vary from one product to another within a group and with the concentration of the disinfectant.

Environmental disinfectants

Phenolics

Table 1 gives the suggested use-dilutions of a selection of phenolic disinfectants for situations of low organic soiling (clean) and high organic soiling (dirty).

(a) Clear soluble phenolics

Examples. This group includes Hycolin, Stericol and Clearsol.

Properties. The properties of clear soluble phenolics are as follows:
- Wide range of bactericidal activity, including tubercle bacilli
- Poor activity against bacterial spores
- Good fungicidal activity; variable virucidal activity, usually poor against non-enveloped viruses
- Not readily inactivated by organic matter
- Incompatible with cationic detergents
- Absorbed by rubber and plastics
- Contact with skin should be avoided
- Taint food; do not use on food preparation surfaces or on equipment that may come into contact with skin or mucous membranes, particularly of infants
- Contain detergents
- Concentrates are stable but stability is reduced on dilution
- Cheap and used for environmental disinfection but increasingly being replaced by chlorine-based agents
- Agent of choice for mycobacteria, including *M. tuberculosis*, in the environment.

Table 1 **Suggested use-dilutions of phenolic disinfectants**

Disinfectant	Manufacturer	Disinfectant concentration:	
		'clean' conditions	'dirty' conditions
		% v/v	% v/v
Clearsol	Coventry Chemicals	0.625	1.0
Hycolin	William Pearson	1.0	2.0
Stericol	Sterling Medicare	1.0	2.0
Izal	Sterling Medicare	1.0	2.0

(b) Black/white fluids

Examples. This group includes Jeyes Fluid, Lysol and Izal.

Properties. The properties are generally similar to those of clear soluble phenolics. Black/white fluids are cheaper than the latter, but have the disadvantage of being more harmful to skin, messy and strong smelling.

(c) Chloroxylenol (4-chloro-3,5-xylenol; 'PCMX')

Examples. This group is exemplified by Dettol.

Properties. The properties of chloroxylenols are as follows:
- Adequate activity against Gram-positive bacteria, but poor activity against some Gram-negative bacteria which can be improved by the addition of chelating agents such as EDTA
- Readily inactivated by a wide range of materials
- Non-corrosive and non-irritant
- Not recommended for environmental or instrument use in hospitals.

Chlorine-based disinfectants

(a) Hypochlorites

Examples. This group includes Chloros, Domestos and Milton.

Properties. The properties of hypochlorites are as follows:

- Wide range of bactericidal, virucidal, sporicidal and fungicidal activity
- Sporicidal, particularly if buffered at around pH 7.6
- Disinfectant of choice for use against viruses, including HIV and HBV (See Table 2)
- Active against mycobacteria at high concentrations (e.g. 5000 p.p.m. available chlorine)
- Rapid action
- Inactivated by organic matter, particularly if used in low concentrations
- Corrosive to some metals
- Incompatible with cationic detergents
- Diluted solutions are unstable and should be freshly prepared daily
- Decomposition is accelerated by light, heat and heavy metals
- Care should be taken not to mix strong acids with hypochlorite because chlorine gas will be released
- Should not be used in the presence of formaldehyde as one of the reaction products is carcinogenic
- High concentrations are caustic and corrosive but low concentrations are non-toxic
- Useful for water treatment and in food preparation areas and milk kitchens
- Useful as a laboratory disinfectant, especially against viruses
- Cheap.

Table 2 **Uses of hypochlorite and strengths of solution**

Use	Dilution of stock solution	Available chlorine	
		%	p.p.m.
	Undiluted	10*	100 000*
Blood spills	1 in 10	1.0	10 000
Laboratory discard	1 in 40	0.25	2500
Environmental disinfection	1 in 100	0.1	1000
Disinfection of clean instruments	1 in 200	0.05	500
Infant feeding utensils, catering surfaces and equipment	1 in 800	0.0125	125

* Approximate values of some brands: Chloros, Sterite, Domestos, etc.

(b) Sodium dichloroisocyanurates (NaDCC)

Examples.　This group includes Presept, Sanichlor, Haz-Tab, Biospot, Titan, Diversey Detergent Sanitizer; may be in the form of tablets, powders or granules.

Properties.　The properties of sodium dichloroisocyanurates are as for hypochlorites, but are more resistant to inactivation by organic matter, slightly less corrosive to metals and often more convenient than hypochlorites. Undissolved tablets, powder and granules are very stable when stored dry but unstable when in solution.

Hydrogen peroxide and peroxygen compounds

Examples.　This group includes peracetic acid, hydrogen peroxide and Virkon.

Properties.　The properties of hydrogen peroxide and peroxygen compounds are as follows:
- Wide range of bactericidal, virucidal and fungicidal activity
- Activity is greatly reduced by organic matter
- Sporicidal activity is variable (peracetic acid has good sporicidal activity)
- Mycobactericidal activity is variable
- Corrosive to some metals

- Often formulated with a detergent
- Hydrogen peroxide and Virkon have low toxicity and irritancy
- Peracetic acid is highly irritant
- Peroxygen compounds (where of low irritancy) are sometimes used for disinfecting small spills and for laboratory equipment where other methods are impractical
- Manufacturer's approval should be obtained before using on equipment where corrosion may present problems (e.g. endoscopes, centrifuges, etc.)

Skin disinfectants

Biguanides (chlorhexidine)

Examples. This group includes Hibiscrub, Hibitane and Savlon (a chlorhexidine/cetrimide mixture). (Many different branded preparations are now available, but the activity of a particular concentration may vary depending on the preparation.)

Properties. The properties of biguanides are as follows:
- More active against Gram-positive than Gram-negative organisms
- No activity against tubercle bacilli
- No activity against bacterial spores
- Good fungicidal activity
- Limited activity against viruses
- Low toxicity and irritancy
- Inactivated by organic matter, soap and anionic detergents
- Most useful as disinfectants for skin and mucous membranes, but should not come into contact with brain, meninges, or middle-ear
- Mixtures of chlorhexidine and cetrimide are available pre-diluted and sterile in single-use sachets; commonly used for cleaning dirty wounds.

Alcohols

Examples. This group includes ethanol (including industrial methylated spirits) and isopropanol.

Properties. The properties of alcohols include the following:

- Good bactericidal (including tubercle bacilli) and fungicidal activity; not sporicidal
- Ethanol is effective against most categories of virus; isopropanol is not effective, ethanol is less effective against non-enveloped viruses
- Rapid action
- Volatile and especially useful as rapidly drying disinfectants for skin and surfaces
- Usual concentrations are 70% for ethanol (90% for viruses) and 60–70% for isopropanol
- Must be used diluted before use (100% alcohol is not an effective disinfectant)
- Do not penetrate well into organic matter, especially protein-based, and should be used only on physically clean surfaces
- Flammable: care should be taken when using alcohols for environmental disinfection or on skin prior to diathermy or on electrical equipment
- Can be used as a base for other bactericides such as chlorhexidine, iodine and triclosan for pre-operative skin disinfection
- Alcohol-impregnated wipes are available for skin prior to injection. These are also used for disinfection of clean surfaces, though this allows limited exposure of the surface to disinfectant and immersion is preferable.

Iodine, iodophors and other iodine preparations

Examples. This group includes aqueous iodine, tincture of iodine, Betadine, Disadine, Videne and Phoraid.

Properties. The properties of iodine, iodophors and other iodine preparations include the following:
- Wide range of bactericidal, virucidal, and fungicidal activity. Some activity against bacterial spores
- Inactivated by organic matter (depending on preparation and concentration)
- May corrode metals
- Tincture of iodine and aqueous iodine solutions can cause skin reactions
- Iodophors (e.g. Betadine, Disadine, Videne) and other iodine compounds (e.g. Phoraid) are complexes of iodine and carrier molecules. The most common carrier molecule is the polymer polyvinyl pyrrolidone, complexes of which are known as povidone- or PVP-iodine. They do not stain skin and are non-irritant.

Hexachlorophane

Examples. This group includes Ster-Zac DC and Ster-Zac powder.

Properties. The properties of hexachlorophane include the following:
- More active against Gram-positive than Gram-negative bacteria
- Little other microbicidal activity
- Bacterial contamination of aqueous solutions can be a problem
- Cutaneously absorbed hexachlorophane may be toxic to babies after repeated application of 3% hexachlorophane emulsions
- Powders containing 0.33% hexachlorophane give some protection against colonisation with *Staphylococcus aureus* in neonates, without significant toxicity risk
- Good residual effect on skin
- Can be used by adults for surgical hand-disinfection or during staphylococcal outbreaks.

Triclosan

Examples. This group includes Manusept, Aquasept, Ster-Zac Bath Concentrate, pHiso-MED, ZalClense and Cidal.

Properties. Triclosan disinfectants have properties and a range of activity similar to hexachlorophane disinfectants. Triclosan disinfectants exhibit no toxicity in neonates.

Quaternary ammonium compounds (QACs) and ampholytic compounds

Examples. This group includes Roccal, Zephiran, Dettol ED, Cetavlon and Tego.

Properties. The properties of QACs include the following:

- More active against Gram-positive than Gram-negative bacteria
- No activity against bacterial spores
- No activity against tubercle bacilli at usual concentrations
- Good fungicidal activity
- Variable activity against viruses
- Bacteriostatic rather than bactericidal at low concentrations
- Inactivated by soaps, anionic detergents and organic matter
- Contamination and growth of Gram-negative bacilli in dilute solutions is possible
- All have some detergent properties
- Sterile QAC solutions with or without chlorhexidine may be used for cleaning dirty wounds
- Some used in catering areas, but not recommended for general use in hospitals
- Ampholytic compounds, e.g. Tego, have properties similar to those of QACs. Mainly used in catering areas and industry.

Disinfectants for instruments

Aldehydes

(a) Glutaraldehyde

Examples. This group includes Cidex, Asep and Totacide.

Properties. The properties of glutaraldehyde include the following:

- Wide range of bactericidal, virucidal and fungicidal activity
- Good but slow activity against bacterial spores
- Active against tubercle bacilli, but less so against *M. avium-intracellulare*
- Irritant to eyes, skin and respiratory mucosa (see occupational exposure standards, pp. 24–25)
- Most preparations are non-corrosive to metals and other materials
- Little inactivation by organic matter, but penetrates slowly
- A good fixative. Prior cleaning is always required
- Alkaline solutions are activated before use and have a limited useful life (14–28 days)
- Acidic solutions do not require activation and are stable, but slower in activity than alkaline buffered solutions
- A useful disinfectant for equipment that cannot be heat-sterilised, such as endoscopes, but it is expensive and toxic. (See occupational exposure standards, pp. 24–25.)

(b) Formaldehyde

Formaldehyde is used mainly as a gaseous fumigant (see p. 53). The humidity, temperature and formaldehyde concentration must be carefully controlled if fumigation is to be effective. Formaldehyde solution is too irritant to be used as a general disinfectant. (See occupational exposure standards, pp. 24–25.)

(c) Other aldehydes

Other aldehydes, such as succine dialdehyde (Gigasept), usually have properties similar to glutaraldehyde, but may not require a buffer. Activity depends mainly on aldehyde concentration.

Other compounds

Other compounds such as alcohols, peroxygen compounds, peracetic acid, and quaternary ammonium compounds (QACs), e.g. Dettol ED, may sometimes be used for the disinfection of instruments (see details given under appropriate headings) but most have disadvantages in microbicidal range, capacity or corrosion. A careful assessment should be made that includes the equipment manufacturer's acceptance of instrument compatibility.

ORGANISMS OF
SPECIAL SIGNIFICANCE

Spores

Some bacteria, such as clostridia, produce spores that are resistant to most disinfectants in common use and may survive boiling. Incineration, autoclaving and dry heat are the most reliable methods of killing bacteria. Two per cent alkaline glutaraldehyde can kill one million spores of *Bacillus subtilis* in 2–3 h, although sometimes 10 h is recommended, based on results of the official test used in the USA (AOAC test). Spores of *Clostridium difficile* are relatively sensitive to 2% glutaraldehyde. Hypochlorite solutions buffered to pH 7.6 are more rapidly sporicidal than glutaraldehyde but may damage instruments. It is important to kill or remove spores on surgical instruments and equipment that comes into contact with a break in the skin or mucous membrane or is introduced into a normally sterile cavity. Disinfection of the environment of patients infected with spore-bearing organisms is unnecessary. Fungal spores are readily killed by disinfectants.

Mycobacteria

Tubercle bacilli (*Mycobacterium tuberculosis*) and other mycobacteria are more resistant to chemical disinfectants than other vegetative bacteria, but less so than spores. Items contaminated with discharges from tuberculous patients should be disposed of by incineration or autoclaving whenever possible. Exposure to water at a temperature of 70°C or above for 5–10 min, or less in a washer–disinfector, 2% alkaline glutaraldehyde or 1–2% clear soluble phenolic disinfectant (depending on the product) for 20 min should kill tubercle bacilli. Some mycobacteria, such as *M. avium-intracellulare* are more resistant to chemical disinfectants than *M. tuberculosis*. Exposure to glutaraldehyde for at least 1 h (preferably 2 h) is recommended if atypical mycobacterial infection is suspected or is likely, for example in AIDS patients. A phenolic disinfectant may be used for disinfecting surfaces. In the post-mortem room, 10% formalin may be introduced into the lungs of suspect tuberculous cadavers (after bacteriological samples have been taken) before commencing the examination. Lungs to be retained for further examination must be immersed in 10% formalin in a sealable container.

Viruses

Hepatitis B virus (HBV) and human immunodeficiency virus (HIV) are inactivated by the usual methods of sterilisation and by boiling water for 5–10 min. HIV is an enveloped virus and available evidence suggests that it should be inactivated by most disinfectants and at temperatures achievable in washing machines, i.e. 70–80°C. The lower temperatures required to inactivate HBV are unknown, but thorough washing and exposure to temperatures between 70–80°C should reduce the risks of transmission.

Two per cent alkaline glutaraldehyde or chlorine-based agents (10 000 p.p.m. available chlorine) will inactivate viruses including HIV in about 1–2 min. 70% alcohol is also effective on clean surfaces. Non-enveloped viruses are relatively resistant to isopropanol and more resistant to ethanol than are enveloped viruses; 85–90% ethanol should be used after thorough cleaning if activity against non-enveloped viruses is required. Phenolics and quaternary ammonium compounds show varying virucidal activity and are not recommended for routine disinfection against viruses. Other agents such as peroxygen compounds and peracetic acid show virucidal activity and may sometimes be considered as an alternative to glutaraldehyde or chlorine-based agents, provided that they do not damage the surfaces, equipment or instruments and appropriate virucidal tests have been carried out.

Viruses causing Lassa and other haemorrhagic fevers are killed by heat, 2% glutaraldehyde and chlorine-based agents. The terminal disinfection of wards, other premises and ambulances after possible contamination with these agents is described elsewhere (DHSS, 1986).

Rabies virus is similarly killed by heat, glutaraldehyde and chlorine-based agents (DHSS, 1977).

Creutzfeldt–Jakob disease is believed to be caused by a 'slow virus' or 'prion', but the agent has not been identified or cultured *in vitro*. It is difficult to inactivate by heat or chemical disinfection. Autoclaving at a temperature between 134–136°C for 18 min (i.e. six routine 3 min cycles) or exposure to a hypochlorite solution (10 000 p.p.m. available chlorine) for 30 min should be effective. Immersion in 1M sodium hydroxide for 1 h is also claimed to be effective. Glutaraldehyde and formaldehyde do not appear to inactivate the agent. Formaldehyde increases resistance to heat, so particular care is needed in handling preserved specimens. Hypochlorite solution or sodium dichloroisocyanurate granules are used for dealing with spills in the environment.

Other organisms

Most of the other organisms causing substantial problems in recent years, such as listeria, campylobacter, legionella, and methicillin-resistant *Staph. aureus*, are all killed by the usual concentrations of disinfectants and heat at temperatures between 70–80°C. Biocides are available that will kill legionella, as well as algae and protozoa associated with them, in cooling towers and storage tanks (DHSS, 1989). Cysts of protozoa, e.g. cryptosporidium, are killed by heat at temperatures between 70–80°C but tend to be resistant to disinfectants in common use such as aldehydes and the low-chlorine concentrations and realistic immersion times required for the decontamination of equipment (DHSS, 1990). Although this could be a problem with gastroscopes and colonoscopes, particularly if used on immuno-compromised patients such as those with AIDS, thorough cleaning by, for example, two to three cycles on an automated endoscope cleaner–disinfector should reduce the risks of transmission considerably.

References

DEPARTMENT OF HEALTH AND SOCIAL SECURITY. 1977. *Memorandum on rabies*. London: HMSO.
DEPARTMENT OF HEALTH AND SOCIAL SECURITY. 1986. *Memorandum on the control of viral haemorrhagic fevers*, London: HMSO.

DEPARTMENT OF HEALTH AND SOCIAL SECURITY. 1989. Report of the Expert *Advisory Committee on Biocides.* London: HMSO

DEPARTMENT OF HEALTH AND SOCIAL SECURITY. 1990. *Report of the Group of Experts. Cryptosporidium in water supplies.* London: HMSO.

SAFETY IN CHEMICAL DISINFECTION

Control of Substances Hazardous to Health (COSHH) Regulations (1988)

The Regulations

The Control of Substances Hazardous to Health Regulations 1988 (COSHH) is the most recent safety legislation to affect the way that disinfectants are selected and used in the UK. These Regulations require all employers to evaluate risks to health for all their employees from exposure to hazardous substances at work. This includes not only chemical disinfectants themselves but the hazards they are supposed to eliminate, i.e. pathogenic micro-organisms. Thus chemical disinfectants in hospitals under COSHH are both a problem and a remedy.

The general philosophy of the COSHH Regulations is that procedures, rather than substances, should be assessed for risk. This takes into account the substance, the nature of its use, the likely exposure of people to the substance and measures taken to limit that exposure. Thus the use of an alcohol skin wipe, for example, would not pose the same risk as a chemical tanker transporting several thousand litres of alcohol. The emphasis of the Regulations is on prevention of exposure to hazardous substances. Personal protective equipment such as gloves, respiratory and eye protection, aprons, etc. should only be used to prevent exposure as a last resort. The employer must also take steps to monitor the correct and safe working of the various protective measures and procedures. Where necessary, the exposure of employees and others who may be exposed should be monitored. The employer also has a duty to 'inform, instruct and train' employees and non-employees on his premises in relevant safety matters. This will include the use of chemical disinfectants.

Exposure to chemical disinfectants can be through direct contact with skin, mucous membranes or by inhalation. Inhalation exposure has two types of control limit: a maximum exposure limit (MEL) and an occupational exposure standard (OES).

An MEL is the maximum concentration of an airborne substance, averaged over a reference period, to which employees may be exposed by inhalation under any circumstances.

An OES is the concentration of an airborne substance, averaged over a reference period, at which, according to current knowledge, there is no evidence that it is likely to be injurious to employees if they are exposed, day after day to the concentration.

It is important to control both short-term and long-term exposure to avoid both types of effect and so both types of exposure limit are listed. The long-term exposure limit is concerned with the total intake over long periods (an 8 h time-weighted average) and is therefore appropriate for protecting against the effects of long-term exposure. The short-term exposure limit (usually 10 min) is aimed primarily at avoiding acute effects, or at least reducing the risk of their occurrence. Specific short-term exposure limits are listed for those substances for which there is evidence of a risk of acute effects occurring as a result of brief exposures. For those substances for which no short-term exposure limit is listed, it is recommended that a figure of three times the long-term exposure limit averaged over a 10 min period be used as a guideline for controlling short-term exposure.

COSHH and chemical disinfectants

The risk from chemicals must be assessed with reference to the toxic properties of that chemical, the amount handled and the manner of its use. A chemical that is extremely hazardous in its concentrated form, chlorine for example, may be beneficial and safe when used in a diluted, controlled manner as in swimming pool disinfection, producing minor irritation at most. Thus chemical disinfectants present two levels of risk. The greater risk is from undiluted disinfectants and should be assessed separately from the diluted preparations. Concentrated disinfectants should always be stored and handled with care. The original container should be the safest storage vessel, designed to minimise any risks that the disinfectant may pose such as flammability or build up of pressure. It should be clearly labelled with the nature of any hazards. Both these advantages may be lost if the disinfectant is decanted or repackaged.

Minimising the manipulation of concentrated solutions reduces the risk of uncontrolled exposure. Splashes and spills occur most frequently on pouring concentrated solutions: the fewer times this happens, the less accidents will occur. Where necessary, personal protective equipment should be used when manipulating concentrated disinfectants. This should be chosen with regard to the areas of the operator's body that are at risk of exposure, their susceptibility to the agent and consideration of the nature of the hazard. Thus where the risk is of vapour inhalation, a surgical mask will play no protective role as it provides no barrier to gaseous chemicals; it would, however, provide some protection against liquid splashes. Similarly, gloves must be chosen with consideration of their chemical resistances and permeabilities.

Safety data sheets are available from disinfectant manufacturers and should be kept with other COSHH assessment data.

Occupational exposure standards

The occupational exposure standard (OES) or maximum exposure limit (MEL) for a number of disinfectants is given below, together with safety notes. The data are taken from EH40/92: Health and Safety Executive.

Disinfectant	Exposure standard (OES) or maximum limit (MEL) (see notes)	Hazards and precautions
Phenol	OES: 10 p.p.m./38 mg m^{-3}, 10 min; 5 p.p.m./19 mg m^{-3}, 8 h	Can be absorbed through skin
Chlorine (hypochlorite solution, sodium dichloroiso-cyanurate (NaDCC))	OES: 1 p.p.m./3 mg m^{-3}, 10 min; 0.5 p.p.m./1.5 mg m^{-3}, 8 h	Do not mix with strong acids; store concentrated liquids in pressure-release containers. If used frequently in poorly-ventilated areas, may cause irritation of eyes and lungs. NaDCC is more likely than alkaline sodium hypochlorite to produce irritating levels of chlorine, e.g. when used to disinfect some urine spills that may be slightly acidic
Hydrogen peroxide	OES: 2 p.p.m./3 mg m^{-3}, 10 min; 1 p.p.m./1.5 mg m^{-3}, 8 h	Strong solutions may be irritant to skin and mucous membranes. High-pressure can develop in sealed containers
Isopropanol (propan-2-ol)	OES: 500 p.p.m./1225 mg m^{-3}, 10 min; 400 p.p.m./980 mg m^{-3}, 8 h	Flammable; can be absorbed through skin
Ethanol (ethyl alcohol)	OES: 1000 p.p.m./1900 mg m^{-3}, 8 h only	May cause eye and skin irritation if used in large quantities in an enclosed space

Disinfectant	Exposure standard (OES) or maximum limit (MEL) (see notes)	Hazards and precautions
Iodine (alcoholic solution, 'tincture', and as solution in potassium iodide, 'Lugol's')	OES: 0.1 p.p.m./1 mg m^{-3}, 10 min only	Can cause skin and eye irritation
Formaldehyde	MEL: 2 p.p.m./2.5 mg m^{-3}, 10 min and 8 h	Potential eye and nasal irritant; causes respiratory distress and allergic dermatitis; respiratory irritation has been observed at 0.2-0.3 p.p.m.; gloves, goggles and aprons should be worn when preparing and disposing of formaldehyde solutions
Glutaraldehyde	OES: 0.2 p.p.m./0.7 mg m^{-3}, 10 min only	Eye and nasal irritant that can cause sensitisation, e.g. asthma,dermatitis. Should be used only in well-ventilated areas. Sensitised individuals can experience respiratory symptoms at concentrations well below the OES. Avoid skin contact. Gloves and goggles should be worn when handling bulk solutions. Latex gloves are sufficient only for brief exposures. Nitrile gloves offer longer term protection.

Notes: Maximum exposure limits (MELs) are the time-weighted average upper limits of a substance permitted in the breathing zone of a person. They are expressed as either parts per million (p.p.m.) or milligrams per cubic metre (mg m^{-3}). Occupational exposure standards (OESs) are the maximum concentrations of a substance in air to which individuals may be exposed during their working life without causing ill-effect. They are often the same as 8 h MELs.

Disinfectants listed elsewhere in this book but not included in this table are of no significant or unusual hazard.

DISINFECTION POLICY

Purpose

The purpose of a policy is to ensure that those responsible for disinfection are familiar with the agents to be used and the procedures involved.

The policy should be useful to all grades of staff and should improve co-operation between disciplines, e.g. nursing and domestic. It should define and standardise the methods (e.g. sterilisation, disinfection and cleaning) for decontamination of equipment, of skin and of the environment. It should also ensure that the same disinfectants and concentrations are used for similar purposes throughout the hospital. The policy should reduce costs by eliminating unnecessary use of disinfectants and, by restricting the number of types available, should allow larger bulk purchases to be made at lower costs.

Organisation and staff training

The hospital infection control committee is responsible for the formulation of the hospital policy, and the microbiologist, head MLSO and safety officer for the laboratory policy. The infection control committee should include the microbiologist, who will usually be the infection control officer/doctor, the infection control nurse and the pharmacist. It is also advisable to include representatives of the users and a purchasing officer in discussions if disinfectants are ordered by the supplies department.

The nursing and domestic staff should be trained in the use of disinfectants by the infection control nurse, pharmacist or the microbiologist. Laboratory staff should be trained by the microbiologist, head MLSO, or a suitably experienced training or safety officer.

The infection control nurse should ensure that all relevant departments are aware of the policy and should monitor its use. An occasional audit of knowledge of staff and use of disinfectants should be made in all wards and units. It is particularly important that new nursing staff are made aware of the policy and that training courses are available for domestic, catering, mortuary and laboratory staff. The importance of using correct dilutions, avoiding splashes to the skin and the wearing of appropriate types of glove when necessary should be stressed.

Formulation of a policy

The formulation of a disinfection policy involves the following steps:

List the purposes for which disinfectants are commonly used, e.g. environment, instruments, skin and mucous membrane.

Eliminate the use of disinfectants where other methods are more appropriate, i.e.:
• Where sterilisation is essential, e.g. surgical instruments, implants, dressings and needles
• Where heat can be used, e.g. washer–disinfectors for dirty surgical instruments, holloware, linen, crockery and cutlery, bedpans and urinals
• Where cleaning alone is adequate, e.g. floors, walls and furniture
• Where single-use items can be used economically, e.g. catheters, gloves and syringes.

If this cannot be done, select a chemical disinfectant.

Arrange for the disinfectant to be distributed at the correct use-dilution whenever possible. Bacteria will grow in weak solutions; strong solutions are wasteful and may be corrosive. Containers should be marked with the date of issue and the date after which the solution should not be used. Containers should be washed with hot water and, preferably, dried before refilling. In some situations it may be necessary to supply containers of undiluted disinfectants. If so, a suitable measuring device for disinfectant and water is necessary. Sachets and tablets are a useful way of obtaining pre-measured amounts of disinfectant.

Choice of a disinfectant

The following should be considered when choosing a disinfectant:
- It should have a wide range of microbicidal activity and, if used for surface disinfection, should be rapid in action
- It should not be readily neutralised by organic matter, soaps, hard water or plastics
- It should be relatively non-corrosive at use-dilutions
- It should be non-irritant if to be applied to the skin
- It should be inexpensive.

A single disinfectant will not fulfil all these requirements, but usually a chlorine-based agent and a clear soluble phenolic will be sufficient for environmental disinfection. Disinfectants such as quaternary ammonium compounds or pine fluids that have a narrow range of microbicidal activity should be avoided. Two per cent glutaraldehyde may be needed for disinfection of medical instruments, particularly endoscopes, and 70% alcohol may be required for rapid disinfection of some items, e.g. thermometers. Compounds of low toxicity, e.g. chlorhexidine, povidone–iodine or 70% alcohol, may be required for skin disinfection and for equipment likely to come into contact with the skin or mucous membranes.

A typical hospital disinfection policy is summarised in Appendix 1.

CLEANING AND DISINFECTION OF THE ENVIRONMENT, SKIN AND MEDICAL EQUIPMENT

Disinfection of the environment

Washing the floor or other horizontal surface with a detergent will remove 80% of micro-organisms, whereas disinfectants will kill or remove 90–99%. The majority of these organisms are normal skin flora and spores, and are unlikely to be an infection hazard to most patients.

Wards and operating theatres

Floors and surfaces of busy wards become recontaminated rapidly after cleaning, and therefore routine chemical disinfection is of little value. Fogging with a disinfectant is unnecessary, comparatively ineffective and not advised.

Floors of operating theatres should be cleaned at the end of each session. Use of disinfectants is not required, except for the removal of spilt body fluid. Flooring should be rinsed weekly with water to remove residual detergent or disinfectant to maintain antistatic properties if required.

Walls and ceilings are rarely heavily contaminated: cleaning once a year should be adequate in wards and two to four times a year in operating theatres.

Spills should be removed as soon as possible and the area washed with detergent and dried. A spill from a known or suspected infected patient should be removed with a disinfectant, e.g. a chlorine-based agent or phenolic, at the concentration recommended for dirty conditions. If the disinfectant is likely to damage the contaminated surface, such as a carpet, a detergent alone or a disinfectant that does not damage the surface should be used.

It is now common practice to treat all blood and body fluids as an infection hazard and to remove spills with a disinfectant, with care; gloves should be worn. Routine disinfection, however, should only be necessary for blood or blood-stained body fluids in areas of high incidence of HIV or HBV infection and in high-risk departments such as accident and emergency, and drug dependency units. A small blood spill from a known or suspected HIV or HBV patient, or in a high-risk unit, can be decontaminated by the addition of a powder or granules of a chlorine-based agent or peroxygen compound to an equal volume of the spill. The blood/disinfectant mixture can then be safely removed with paper towels after a short interval, e.g. 1–2 min. Larger volumes of blood should be removed with large volumes of a chlorine-based agent (10 000 p.p.m. available chlorine). Care should be taken in using chlorine-based compounds since chlorine gas is released when they come into contact with acid, some cleaning agents, hot water, or urine, particularly if present in large volumes. The main hazard of a blood spill is probably that to the individual dealing with it: the disinfectant should not be relied on to penetrate the spill completely, and gloves should be discarded after use with any solid blood/powder mixtures and paper towels as clinical waste. Plastic aprons should also be worn if large spills are to be removed. Mops and buckets should be disinfected after removal of the spill. Thorough cleaning of the surface and wearing of gloves is more important in preventing infection than the use of a disinfectant in the removal of the spill.

Baths and wash-basins

Thorough cleaning of baths with a detergent after use is usually sufficient. Disinfection of baths and taps may be advisable during outbreaks of infection and after use by infected patients. A non-abrasive chlorine-based powder is commonly recommended, but a solution of chlorine-based agent and a detergent is a possible alternative. Care is necessary to ensure that non-abrasive powders or creams are used on modern baths and that detergents mixed with chlorine-based agents are compatible.

Antiseptic solutions, e.g. Savlon or Ster-Zac for staphylococcal infections, may be added to the bath water of patients with infected lesions to reduce the contamination of the water and reduce deposition of organisms on the surface of the bath; cleaning is still necessary after an antiseptic bath additive has been used. Savlon should not be used with soap as it is inactivated.

Wash-basins should be cleaned not less often than once a day. Heated sink traps are of doubtful value in reducing cross-infection.

Toilets and drains

Toilet seats and handles should be kept clean and washed not less often than once a day; disinfection may be required during outbreaks of infection. A chlorine-based agent or clear soluble phenolic solution may be used for this purpose, but should be rinsed off the seat before use by the next patient. Toilet pans and sink outlets should be cleaned regularly, but disinfection of pans and pouring disinfectants into drains is of no value.

Washing bowls

Washing bowls should be washed, dried and stored inverted. If used by infected patients, bowls may be washed with a phenolic solution or a solution of a chlorine-based agent and then thoroughly rinsed, dried and stored inverted. An individual bowl for each patient may be desirable in high-risk units, e.g. intensive therapy, when it is then terminally disinfected before use by another patient.

Kitchens

Prevention of infection from food is achieved mainly by good hygienic practice, which includes adequate cooking; cleaning and use of dedicated food-preparation surfaces; maintenance of correct refrigeration temperatures; heat rather than chemical disinfection of utensils; and correct storage of foods. Dishwashers should give a final rinse temperature of at least 80°C for 1 min, or for another appropriate temperature and time combination, to ensure disinfection of the load. In the absence of a machine, thorough cleaning, rinsing and drying is adequate for general wards, but single-use crockery and cutlery may be required for patients with untreated tuberculosis, salmonellosis and some other infectious diseases, if a suitable washing machine is unavailable.

Disinfectants should only be used in special circumstances on advice from the microbiologist. Disinfectants suitable for kitchen use are chlorine-based agents (120–200 p.p.m. available chlorine) or, where these might cause corrosion, quaternary ammonium compounds. Surfaces should be cleaned before disinfectants are applied. Phenolic disinfectants should not be used in kitchens as they may taint food even at very low concentrations. Hand disinfectants (chlorhexidine, povidone–iodine or triclosan) are rarely necessary and should only be used on advice from the microbiologist. Use of nail-brushes should be avoided if possible since they damage the skin. If used, they should be disinfected regularly by heat.

Cleaning equipment

Although not a major source or route of infection, cleaning equipment should be kept clean and stored dry. Vacuum cleaners should be fitted with efficient filters, and exhausts should be directed away from the floor. Oiled or dust-attracting mops reduce the dispersal of dust, provided that the mop heads are changed regularly, e.g. every two days. Brooms, which raise dust, should not be used.

Wet floor-mops should be rinsed after use and dried. If necessary, they can be disinfected by immersion for 30 min in a hypochlorite (1000 p.p.m. available chlorine) or a phenolic solution after preliminary cleaning. Prolonged storage in a phenolic solution is inadvisable as disinfectant-resistant Gram-negative bacilli may be selected; phenolic solutions may be partially inactivated by plastic mop-heads. Autoclaving, or disinfection in a washing-machine, is preferable, particularly for mops used in operating theatres. Mop buckets should be cleaned and stored inverted. Scrubbing machines should be designed so that tanks can be emptied, cleaned and dried.

Disinfection of the skin and mucous membranes

Introduction

The micro-organisms on the skin can, for practical purposes, be classified as 'residents' or 'transients'. The 'resident' flora, mainly coagulase-negative staphylococci and diphtheroids, grow on the skin and not all can be removed by washing or disinfection. The 'transient' flora are organisms deposited on the skin but do not usually grow there, e.g. *Escherichia coli*, and can be readily removed by washing or disinfection. Some organisms, e.g. *Klebsiella* spp. and *Staph. aureus* may occasionally survive and grow on the hands for several days or longer and are often described as temporary residents. *Staph. aureus* frequently colonises the anterior nares and less commonly other areas of the skin such as the perineum. *Acinetobacter* spp. are the only Gram-negative bacilli which colonise certain areas of skin and can be described as true residents. *Staph. aureus* and Gram-negative bacilli may colonise damaged or eczematous skin.

Hand washing and disinfection

Bacteria or viruses carried transiently on the hands are a cross-infection hazard to susceptible patients in wards. Washing with soap or detergent for 15–20 s is generally effective in removing transient micro-organisms, provided that an effective technique is used. Special attention should be paid to the tips of the fingers, the thumbs and other areas of the hands likely to contact a contaminated site. A defined method of washing is advised (Figure 1). If heavily contaminated materials are handled it is advisable to wear gloves in addition to washing the hands. Detergent preparations containing an antiseptic, e.g. chlorhexidine or povidone–iodine, are often recommended for use during outbreaks of infection and sometimes routinely in special units such as neonatal intensive care. Drying of hands is important and good quality paper towels should be used. Hot-air driers are effective but slow and are usually noisy. They are suitable for use in certain areas such as washrooms and public toilets, but their use in clinical areas is not advisable.

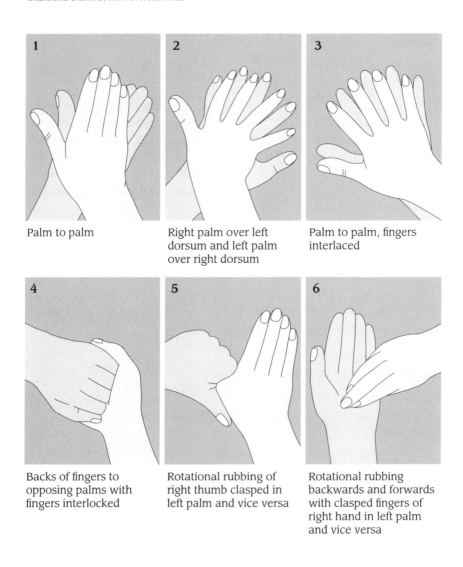

1 Palm to palm

2 Right palm over left dorsum and left palm over right dorsum

3 Palm to palm, fingers interlaced

4 Backs of fingers to opposing palms with fingers interlocked

5 Rotational rubbing of right thumb clasped in left palm and vice versa

6 Rotational rubbing backwards and forwards with clasped fingers of right hand in left palm and vice versa

Apply 3–5 mL of the formulation to the cupped hands and carry out steps 1–6 one or more times using the following procedure. Each step consists of three strokes (routine or hygienic hand-disinfection) or five strokes (surgical hand-disinfection) backwards and forwards. (See also Ayliffe GAJ, *et al.*, 1978; Lawrence JC, 1985.)

Figure 1 **Hand washing and disinfection technique**

An alternative and more effective method of hand disinfection is the application of 70% (85–90% for enteroviruses) ethanol or 60–70% isopropanol, with or without an added disinfectant, and containing an emollient, e.g. 1% glycerol. The hands and fingers are rubbed together with about 3 mL of the mixture until dry, ensuring that all surfaces are covered as described above. This method provides a convenient, rapid and effective alternative to hand washing in situations where there is no gross soiling of the hands or where a sink is not readily available. This method can be introduced temporarily into a unit during an outbreak of infection or as a routine hand preparation prior to some aseptic techniques.

The use of a skin disinfectant, either an antiseptic-detergent or an alcoholic rub, for removing or killing transient flora on the hands is often referred to as 'hygienic hand-disinfection', although in some European countries the term implies disinfection with an alcoholic solution and usually excludes removal by washing.

Surgical hand-disinfection

Surgical hand-disinfection requires the removal or killing of transient skin-microflora and a substantial reduction and suppression of the resident population. The active agent must be well tolerated by the user, should produce a high level of kill and should sustain a reduction in the 'resident' flora for the duration of surgery. Similar concentrations of the active agent in different products does not necessarily imply equal effectiveness, so new products should be tested. Preparations that are in current use include 4% chlorhexidine–detergent and a povidone–iodine solution containing 0.75% available iodine. These preparations (or the alternative described below) should be used for all hand washing during operating sessions to achieve a cumulative effect on the 'resident' flora. A sterile nail-brush can be used at the beginning of an operating list to clean the finger nails and remove ingrained dirt. Repeated scrubbing tends to damage the skin and may be associated with an increase in the numbers of resident organisms possibly allowing *Staph. aureus* to colonise the hands. A thorough wash of hands and forearms for 2 min with an antiseptic detergent should be adequate.

A more rapid effect can be obtained with an alcoholic solution (e.g. 0.5% chlorhexidine or triclosan in 60–70% ethanol or isopropanol) rubbed vigorously into hands and forearms until dry. Two applications of 5 mL are recommended.

A single application of the preparation between cases on the operating list should be sufficient. A defined method of application of the agent to the hands should be used.

User acceptability

Any preparations used for hand washing or disinfection must be acceptable to the user and not damage the skin on repeated use. If the preparation is not accepted by staff it will not be used. Damaged skin will increase the number of resident bacteria and may become heavily colonised with *Staph. aureus.*

Injection sites

The necessity to disinfect the skin with 70% ethanol or 60–70% iso-propanol before injection is controversial. There is evidence that giving an injection without prior disinfection is not associated with increased infection risk in young, healthy individuals; prior disinfection is not recommended for routine insulin injections in diabetic patients because of potential damage to the skin. Some hospitals have stopped using alcohol for disinfection of injection sites and no adverse effects have been reported. It is still used (usually with chlorhexidine) before cannulation procedures, intra-articular injections and taking blood cultures. However, disinfection of the injection site continues to be used in most hospitals particularly for injections into the thigh and in elderly or immunocompromised patients or close to infected or colonised lesions. The area should be wiped thoroughly and allowed to dry before the injection is given. This will remove or kill most 'transient' organisms.

Pre-operative disinfection of patients' skin and mucous membranes

As for surgical scrubs, agents used for pre-operative disinfection of the patient's skin should be active mainly against the 'resident' flora. The final preparation to be used on the operation site must be rapidly acting and have a prolonged antibacterial effect. Alcoholic solutions of 0.5% chlorhexidine, povidone–iodine containing 1% available iodine, or 1% iodine or 0.5% triclosan are most frequently used, although 1% iodine in 70% ethanol and potassium iodide can give rise to skin reactions. Alcoholic solutions must be allowed to dry thoroughly before the operation, especially if diathermy or electrocautery is to be used.

A high cumulative reduction in 'residents' can be obtained by repeated use of chlorhexidine or hexachlorophane detergents before the operation. However, the effect of two or three chlorhexidine baths or showers on the clean wound infection rate has shown variable results. A single bath with chlorhexidine is unlikely to influence the infection rate in general surgery. A thorough single application of an alcoholic solution to the operating site is as, or more, effective in reducing the resident flora than repeated application of an antiseptic detergent.

Where there is ingrained dirt or where spores on the skin present a special hazard, washing with detergents or grease-solvent gels, e.g. Swarfega, followed by application of an aqueous povidone–iodine compress (containing 1% available iodine) for at least 30 min will reduce the number of spores, but prophylactic penicillin should still be given to patients thought to be at risk from gas gangrene.

Applications of aqueous solutions of chlorhexidine or povidone–iodine are effective for disinfection of oral mucous membranes. A vaginal douche of 0.5% povidone–iodine, containing 0.05% available iodine, e.g. a 5% solution of aqueous Betadine, followed by use of povidone–iodine vaginal gel, can be used for disinfection of the vaginal mucosa. A 1% chlorhexidine cream instilled into the urethra will disinfect this site before cystoscopy or catheterisation.

Treatment of staphylococcal carriers

It is not necessary to treat nasal carriers of *Staph. aureus*, unless the strain is causing infection in the carriers themselves or in others. An antibacterial cream containing 0.5% neomycin and 0.1% chlorhexidine (Naseptin), or a suitable alternative, e.g. one containing neomycin-bacitracin or 1% chlorhexidine, should be applied to the anterior nares three or four times a day for one to two weeks and repeated if necessary. Two per cent mupirocin (Bactroban) has been shown to be more effective than other preparations and is particularly useful for treating carriers of methicillin-resistant *Staph. aureus* (MRSA). However, mupirocin resistance has been reported, and if possible its use should be restricted to carriers of MRSA and prolonged use avoided; preferably, it should not be used on skin lesions. Antibiotics used for systemic treatment, e.g. fusidic acid and gentamicin, should not be used topically. Nasal and skin carriers should also wash routinely and bath daily (for at least one week) with an antiseptic detergent that contains, for example, chlorhexidine, povidone–iodine or triclosan.

Prevention of staphylococcal colonisation in neonates

Selective antibacterial agents have been found useful in preventing colonisation of babies by *Staph. aureus*, while allowing development of a normal 'resident' flora. Application of powders containing hexachlorophane, e.g. Ster-Zac to the umbilicus (normally the primary site of *Staph. aureus* colonisation), groin, buttocks, axillae and lower abdomen reduces the rate of colonisation with *Staph. aureus* while allowing normal colonisation with coagulase-negative staphylococci. The selective colonisation with Gram-negative bacilli on a moist umbilicus is a possible disadvantage. However, the necessity to apply an antiseptic preparation routinely in the absence of staphylococcal infection in the neonatal unit is uncertain and it may be preferable to retain the use of antiseptics only for such problems. Bathing the baby or washing the susceptible areas with 4% chlorhexidine–detergent will also reduce staphylococcal colonisation and is useful during outbreaks of infection.

Disinfection of medical equipment

(See also Table 3, p. 43.)

Respiratory equipment

Mechanical ventilators, humidifiers and associated tubing and equipment are frequently contaminated with *Pseudomonas aeruginosa* or other Gram-negative bacilli. Disinfection of a ventilator after each use is unnecessary provided that it is protected by filters that are impermeable to bacteria. If decontamination is required, autoclaving is preferred, although sterilisation is unnecessary since spore-bearing organisms are not a cause of respiratory infection. Some ventilators have an autoclavable internal circuit, but others can be disinfected with nebulised hydrogen peroxide or formaldehyde gas. The smaller ventilators can often be decontaminated with ethylene oxide or low-temperature steam (LTS). The hazards of infection can also be reduced by lowering the amount of condensation in a circuit by means of heat – moisture exchangers and moisture traps.

The external circuit, and often the humidifiers, can be disinfected in a washing machine at a temperature of at least 71°C for 3 min or 80°C for 1 min, or other appropriate time/temperature combination, or in an LTS machine at 73°C. Disposable circuits can be used but are more expensive. The external circuit should be changed every 48 h or between patients. This can be reduced to weekly or between patients if a heat–moisture exchanger is used. Humidifiers can often be decontaminated by increasing the temperature of the water to 70°C or higher. Humidifiers should be cleaned and dried and refilled with sterile water every 48–72 h. If nebulisers are used, they should be rinsed in alcohol after cleaning if heat disinfection is not possible.

Anaesthetic equipment is contaminated mainly at the face-mask and proximal end of tubing and treatment of the machine is rarely necessary. A filter should be included between the patient and the machine and a disposable circuit employed if the equipment is to be used on a case of open tuberculosis. The circuit should be replaced not less often than once per session, i.e. 10–12 patients, and treated in a washing machine or by LTS after washing; replacement of the circuit after each patient is preferable but clean face-masks should always be provided for each patient.

An appropriate washer–disinfector or LTS machine should be available for treating respiratory equipment. Single-use equipment is too expensive for regular renewal on the basis indicated above. Chemical disinfection by immersion in a chlorine-based agent (e.g. 200 p.p.m. available chlorine) after cleaning, followed by thorough rinsing before reuse is a possible alternative provided that the equipment is not damaged by chlorine. Two per cent glutaraldehyde is too irritant and should not be used for soaking respiratory equipment.

Endoscopes

(See also Table 3.)

Endoscopes, particularly flexible fibre-optic instruments, are difficult to clean because of narrow channels and valves, and often contain heat-labile components. Although such instruments are expensive, the availability of more than one instrument for a session will allow more time for cleaning and disinfection between patients.

Operative endoscopes

Operative endoscopes, e.g. arthroscopes and laparoscopes, should ideally be sterilised, but autoclaving at high temperature is only possible with certain instruments if approved by the manufacturer. Low-temperature steam and formaldehyde or ethylene oxide are acceptable methods of sterilisation, but are not often available for routine use. Immersion in 2% glutaraldehyde for 3 h is an alternative method, but the time available for immersion is usually related to the time interval between patients. A high level of disinfection is usually adequate: the minimum effective immersion time in a disinfectant between use of the endoscope in successive patients is uncertain, but 10–20 min is usually recommended, (20 min is preferable to provide adequate activity against tubercle bacilli). Spores are unlikely to be

Table 3 **Chemical disinfection of medical equipment**

Method and equipment	Immersion time*	Level of decontamination
	min	
2% alkaline glutaraldehyde		
Gastroscopes	4	Disinfection (BSG, 1988)
Bronchoscope	20	Disinfection[†] (BTS, 1989)
	90–120	Disinfection (after known or suspected atypical mycobacteria)
Cystoscopes	10	Disinfection (Cooke *et al.*, 1993)
	20	Disinfection[†]
Arthroscopes, laparoscopes	10	Disinfection
	20	Disinfection[†]
	180	Sterilisation
Other instruments	10	Disinfection
	20	Disinfection[†]
	180	Sterilisation
70% ethanol		
Gastroscopes	4	Disinfection (BSG, 1988)
Other instruments	5–10	Disinfection[†]

* Cleaning to a high standard is essential before disinfection, particularly with 70% ethanol.
[†] Tuberculocidal activity, minimal activity against bacterial spores.

present in other than very small numbers in a well-cleaned endoscope, and pathogenic spores are less resistant to glutaraldehyde than those commonly used for test purposes.

Cystoscopes can be adequately treated by immersion in glutaraldehyde for a minimum of 10–20 min since spore-forming organisms are unlikely to cause urinary tract infection; autoclaving, treatment with LTS or pasteurisation are preferred methods if suitable equipment is available. The newer operative endoscopes are often flexible and will not withstand heat. Suitable washing machines for use with glutaraldehyde are now available but care should be taken to avoid microbial recontamination on rinsing to remove the disinfectant.

All items should be thoroughly cleaned before immersion and invasive instruments must be rinsed in sterile water before reuse.

A closed system, using peracetic acid, is now available and is sporicidal in less than 10 min. It is expensive and does not have a cleaning cycle. Further information on corrosiveness is required and equipment manufacturers' approval should be sought on such compatibility. It may be particularly suitable for cystoscopes and other operative endoscopes.

Flexible endoscopes

Thorough irrigation of all channels (i.e. biopsy, suction, air, water and auxiliary channels) with detergent and disinfectant, followed by thorough rinsing, should be performed between patients. This can be achieved manually using an all-channel irrigation device, although numerous automated machines are now available (see p. 46).

The disinfectant of choice is 2% alkaline glutaraldehyde (e.g. Cidex, Totacide, Asep) or 10% succine dialdehyde (Gigasept) because they have a broad antimicrobial range and do not damage metals, rubber, plastic or lens cement. Most flexible endoscopes are now fully immersible and the internal channels are more accessible. However, glutaraldehyde is a toxic and irritant substance and can give rise to allergic reactions (see occupational exposure standards, pp. 24–25). Other agents such as peracetic acid, peroxygen compounds or QACs followed by alcohol, may be used if their activity is found to be microbiologically acceptable and they do not damage the instrument.

The professional societies in the UK (British Society of Gastroenterology, 1988; British Thoracic Society, 1989; British Association of Urological Surgeons, 1993) have issued recommendations for decontamination.

Gastrointestinal endoscopes

The British Society of Gastroenterology (BSG) has published recommended procedures for the disinfection of gastrointestinal endoscopes. Before starting a list, a routine disinfection cycle of endoscope immersion in 2% glutaraldehyde for 4 min should be sufficient (although the BSG recommend 20 min). Thorough rinsing is always required after disinfection to remove disinfectant residues. Between patients on a list, it is considered sufficient to thoroughly clean endoscopes with detergent and then to immerse them in 2% glutaraldehyde or 10% succine dialdehyde for 4 min to inactivate vegetative bacteria and viruses (including HIV and HBV). An alternative procedure for use by staff sensitised to glutaraldehyde, when infection risk is low, is to clean endoscopes with a detergent or QAC, e.g. Dettol ED, for 2 min, followed by disinfection with 70% ethanol or industrial methylated spirit for 4 min. The period of immersion in alcohol should not exceed 5 min. AIDS patients are managed as immunocompromised and endoscopes and accessory equipment should be treated with 2% alkaline glutaraldehyde for 20 min both before and after the procedure, since mycobacteria may survive on a routinely treated instrument or may be infecting the patient (the BSG recommends 1 h). At the end of a list, prolonged disinfection with aldehyde for 20 min should be carried out. After cleaning, disinfection and rinsing, endoscopes should be dried (preferably with alcohol) before being stored.

Endoscopes should be processed according to the manufacturer's instructions. Cleaning the suction and biopsy channels with a sterilised or disinfected brush is always required, even if an automated cleaning and disinfection machine is used.

Bronchoscopes

Mycobacteria are more resistant than other vegetative bacteria to glutaraldehyde and The British Thoracic Society recommends that bronchoscopes should be thoroughly cleaned and immersed in 2% glutaraldehyde for 20 min between patients and for 1 h after a known or suspected case of pulmonary tuberculosis. However, recent evidence suggests that immersion for 20 min should be sufficient following a known case of pulmonary tuberculosis, provided that the bronchoscope is cleaned thoroughly beforehand. Bronchoscopes should be rinsed in sterile water or 70% alcohol (after tap water) to avoid recontamination with environmental opportunistic mycobacteria. After bronchoscopy on known or suspected infections with *Mycobacterium avium-intracellulare*, a longer immersion time (e.g. 90–120 min) in glutaraldehyde is advised.

Endoscope accessories

All accessories should be cleaned thoroughly, preferably by ultrasonics. Many of the reusable accessories associated with endoscopy, e.g. biopsy forceps, injection needles, water bottles, etc., will now withstand autoclaving, and the use of an SSD tray service or bench-top steriliser is recommended. Alternatively, they may be immersed in glutaraldehyde and rinsed. Single-use accessories can be employed if the costs are acceptable.

Washer–disinfectors

A number of automated machines are now available that can be programmed to clean, disinfect and rinse the internal channels and external surfaces of flexible fibre-optic endoscopes and their accessories. Studies have shown that this equipment can offer a more reliable decontamination process than can be achieved manually. This equipment can also contribute to reducing the exposure of staff to glutaraldehyde.

The machine needs to be convenient to use, effective, non-damaging and sufficiently adaptable to accommodate the range of endoscope equipment held. Furthermore, the user must be able to select a programme that conforms with the national and local policies on disinfection. In some situations a machine that is capable of processing more than one endoscope or a second machine may be required.

The cleaning and disinfection of all channels of endoscopes is important and a thorough rinse is mandatory. The rinse water must be of high microbiological quality and preferably filtered through a bacteria-retaining filter so that the instrument does not become recontaminated. Gram-negative bacilli may be introduced if the water reservoir, or any other part of the machine, is not automatically disinfected during a washing cycle. If this is not possible, a self-disinfection cycle should take place before each session and all the water drained from the machine when not in use. Systems are now available with integral fume extraction. A record must be kept of the number of washing cycles to ensure that the disinfectant is not unreasonably diluted or neutralised by organic matter.

The antimicrobial and cleaning efficacy of a machine can be tested by artificial contamination of the channels of an endoscope with a suspension of a Gram-negative bacillus, e.g. *Pseudomonas aeruginosa* and 10% serum. After drying for 10 min, the channels are individually sampled before and after cleaning and disinfection, and the number of survivors measured. A 100 000-fold reduction (preferably 1 000 000-fold) should be achieved. In-use tests should also be carried out during routine endoscopy sessions by testing rinse water passed through the channels and swabs of the outer surface of the insertion tube for the normal endogenous flora of patients; a minimum of 20 tests is recommended. If a new disinfectant is included, a series of laboratory screening tests could be added such as suspension tests with a range of organisms, including *Pseudomonas aeruginosa, Streptococcus faecalis* and one or two viruses including polio virus; and surface tests with at least one Gram-negative bacillus, *Mycobacterium tuberculosis,* and a virus such as polio virus. A 100 000-fold reduction in 5 min (10–20 min for mycobacteria) is suggested as a possible requirement for laboratory tests.

Use of glutaraldehyde

This agent is potentially hazardous, particularly in endoscopy units and operating theatres (see occupational exposure standards, pp. 24–25). Containers or machines should enclose the aldehyde solutions properly and an air extraction unit or fume cupboard should be provided to reduce the exposure of operators to the vapour. Skin exposure is a greater hazard and operators should avoid skin contact by wearing gloves that are not readily penetrable by glutaraldehyde, e.g. Viton or nitrile, and plastic aprons.

Activated alkaline glutaraldehyde solutions are unstable and should not be used for longer than the period recommended by manufacturers (e.g. 14–28 days). However, the length of time for which a solution remains effective depends also on its dilution and whether it is contaminated with organic materials. The concentration of glutaraldehyde should not fall below 1.5% if the manufacturer's recommended procedures are used. Solutions used in automated machines become diluted more rapidly and should be changed daily, or after 20 endoscopes have been processed. The cleaning of endoscopes such as cystoscopes by hand involves less dilution of disinfectant and, as a guideline, solutions can be changed weekly, or after 100 endoscopes have been processed. The condition of solutions should preferably be monitored by measuring glutaraldehyde concentration. Systems are now available for this to be performed. Rinse water should also be changed frequently to avoid carry over of aldehydes from the disinfection stage and their build up on the instrument, particularly on the eyepieces where the disinfectant will cause eye irritation.

Babies' incubators

Thorough cleaning with a detergent, paying particular attention to the ports, handles and mattresses, followed by drying is usually adequate. If disinfection is required, the surfaces may be wiped with a weak solution of a chlorine-releasing agent (125 p.p.m. available chlorine) and a compatible detergent. Wiping with 70% alcohol after cleaning will disinfect but care is necessary to avoid damage to plastics. Care should be taken to aerate the incubator before reuse. Some humidifiers within the incubator can be disinfected by raising the temperature of the water to over 70°C, or can be removed and autoclaved. Formaldehyde cabinets are also effective, but cleaning is still necessary and care must be taken to aerate to ensure removal of formaldehyde. Formaldehyde disinfectors are expensive and should not be required in most hospitals, but if available should be sited in the hospital's SSD since careful control is required.

Disinfection of laundry

(Hospital laundry arrangements for used and infected linen are covered in detail in DHSS HC(87)30, from which the following advice is taken.)

Linen should be divided into three categories: used (soiled and fouled); infected; and heat-labile. Linen from patients infected with hazard group 4 organisms must be steam sterilised within the hospital before laundering. Disinfection of linen in the first two categories is achieved within the washing process by a combination of high temperature and dilution effects. Heat-labile items must be washed at low temperature (40°C) to avoid shrinkage so their use by patients infected with hazard group 3 organisms should be avoided whenever possible. Where chemical disinfection is considered to be necessary, sodium hypochlorite (150 p.p.m. available chlorine) may be added to the penultimate rinse, which needs to be of not less than 5 min duration. Hypochlorites must not be used on fabrics treated with fire retardants.

References

AYLIFFE GAJ, BABB JR, QUORAISHI AH. 1978. A test for 'hygienic' hand disinfection. *J Clin Path*, **31**, 923-8.

BRITISH SOCIETY OF GASTROENTEROLOGY. 1988. Cleaning and disinfection of equipment for gastro-intestinal flexible endoscopy: interim recommendations of a working party of the British Society of Gastroenterology. *Gut*, **29**, 1134-51.

BRITISH THORACIC SOCIETY. 1989. Bronchoscopy and infection control. *Lancet*, **2**, 270.

COOKE RP, FENELEY RC, AYLIFFE G, LAWRENCE WT, EMMERSON AM, GREENGRASS SM. 1993. Decontamination of urological equipment: interim report of a working group. *Br J Urol,* **71**, 5-9.

DEPARTMENT OF HEALTH AND SOCIAL SECURITY. 1987. Hospital laundry arrangements for used and infected linen. HC(87)30. London: HMSO.

LAWRENCE JC. 1985. The bacteriology of burns. *J Hosp Infect*, **6** (Suppl B), 3-17.

USE OF DISINFECTANTS
IN THE LABORATORY

(See also Health Services Advisory Committee (1991a) which covers use of chemical disinfectants in hospital laboratories in detail and which should be read in conjunction with the following.)

Safe handling of disinfectants

Concentrated solutions of laboratory disinfectants are potentially dangerous and care must be taken in handling them. Concentrated sodium hypochlorite solutions are extremely corrosive, and splashes will bleach clothing. Phenolics are toxic. Glutaraldehyde sensitises the skin and mucous membranes, and formalin vapour is extremely irritant and toxic. (See occupational exposure standards, pp. 24–25). Adequate protective clothing, including appropriate gloves, should be worn when handling concentrated solutions. Splashes on the skin or in the eye must be washed off at once with large volumes of water.

Discard jars

Choice of disinfectant

Clear soluble phenolic fluids are suitable for bacteriological work, and sodium hypochlorite or sodium dichloroisocyanurate (NaDCC) for bacteriological (other than mycobacterial), virological, haematological or biochemical work. Chlorine-based disinfectants are prone to inactivation by organic matter and so hypochlorite-containing discard jars should be checked regularly before discard (see in-use tests, Appendix 2).

Preparation of accurate use-dilutions

Use-dilutions must be prepared accurately in clean containers. The dilutions should be changed daily if heavily used, or in the case of phenolics not less often than once a week if little used. The outside of discard jars should be clearly marked, e.g. with a felt-tip pen, to show the level of an exact volume of water to which should be added the correct volume of disinfectant. Dispensers that deliver a pre-set volume of disinfectant, sachets of disinfectant, or tablets (NaDCC) may be used. Suggested use-dilutions are as follows: Clearsol, 1.0%; Stericol, 2.0%; Hycolin, 2.0%; sodium hypochlorite and NaDCC, 2500 p.p.m. available chlorine.

Treatment of discarded items

Items placed in discard jars must be completely submerged in the disinfectant. The disinfectant must be in contact with all the inner surfaces of the items and with their contents. Items must remain in the disinfectant for at least 1 h and preferably overnight before disposal. The disinfectant must then be emptied down a sink (not a hand wash-basin) through a sieve or colander. Solid waste contaminated with high-risk pathogens must be either incinerated or autoclaved. Solid waste contaminated with low-risk pathogens should be incinerated, autoclaved, or disposed of in sealed plastic bags along with laboratory waste. Reusable pipettes may be washed after overnight submersion without prior autoclaving.

In-use tests

Disinfectants are inactivated to varying extents by many different substances, and a recommended use-dilution is not necessarily effective in all circumstances. Regular in-use testing is therefore recommended. Failures are nearly always caused by inaccurate measurement of use-dilutions, by keeping the disinfectant in use for too long, by adding too much organic material or by a failure to clean a discard jar before refilling. If failures continue after these points have been checked, then the concentration of the use-dilution should be increased, the load in each jar reduced, or an effective physical method of disinfection adopted.

Decontamination of infectious spills

Single-use gloves must be worn for dealing with infectious spills. A spill of this kind can be disinfected by sprinkling a roughly equal volume of chlorine-based granules or peroxygen compound powder over its surface, and it may then be removed with paper towels or a scoop after about 1–2 min. Alternatively, a liquid disinfectant may be used; phenolic disinfectants can be used for bacterial spills. Used towels and cloths, solid or liquid waste and used gloves must be placed in a container for infected waste. Glass fragments must be picked up with forceps, or an autoclavable (or disposable) scoop or dustpan and brush; eye protection must be worn.

Exhaust protective cabinets

After use, the work surface of the cabinet should be washed with a suitable disinfectant; single-use gloves must be worn. A clear soluble phenolic fluid, or chlorine-based agent is suitable after bacteriological work, and a chlorine-based agent after virological, biochemical or haematological work. The cabinet must be fumigated with formaldehyde should a large spill occur and before air grids are cleaned of fluff, filters are changed or any maintenance work is done. More regular fumigation may be required if warranted by the type and volume of work undertaken. The non-return valve on the cabinet exhaust must be closed and the front closure (night door) used when the inside of the cabinet is fumigated by one of the following methods:

Method 1. Add 10 g of potassium permanganate to 35 mL of formalin BP in a 500 mL beaker and immediately seal the cabinet. (The mixture boils rapidly, releasing formaldehyde.) If too much potassium permanganate is added, there is a risk of explosion; if too much formalin is used, a polymer may be deposited in the cabinet and on the filters.

Method 2. Boil 25 mL of formalin BP in a dish on an electric heater that switches off automatically when no more liquid remains.

Method 3. Boil 25 mL of formalin BP in a purpose-built device such as the LEEC Formalin Vaporizer (LEEC Ltd).

The quantities specified here may be increased if larger than usual cabinets are used. After overnight fumigation, the formaldehyde should be exhausted to the outside air by switching on the fan and opening the front closure of the cabinet a few millimetres to allow entry of air. Before doing so, ensure that no one (e.g. window cleaners or engineers) is in the vicinity of the exhaust outlet.

Special equipment

Centrifuges

The routine disinfection of centrifuges is not recommended. However, disinfection may be necessary before service or when tubes break or leak during centrifugation. Following a breakage, the lid should be kept closed (or rapidly reclosed on discovery of the breakage) for at least 30 min to allow aerosols to settle. Protective gloves must be worn, and forceps or swabs held in forceps used to pick up glass debris. Broken glass, buckets, trunnions and the rotor must be autoclaved or placed in a non-corrosive disinfectant (not hypochlorite) known to be effective against the organisms concerned, such as a phenolic, 70% alcohol, or 2% glutaraldehyde, and left for at least 10–20 min. Unbroken, capped tubes may be placed in the disinfectant in a separate container for at least 10–20 min and the contents then recovered. The centrifuge bowl must be swabbed with disinfectant, left to dry, then swabbed again, and finally wiped with water and dried. It is preferable, should glutaraldehyde be used, to carry out disinfection in a fume cupboard or safety cabinet fitted with an exhaust to the external air.

Automated equipment in chemical pathology laboratories

It is generally only necessary to decontaminate the internal surfaces of those parts of the equipment that carry liquids and are in direct contact with samples. The outer surfaces of the equipment require no treatment. For routine cleaning of the liquid flow channels at the end of the working day, flushing with distilled water or the manufacturer's wash fluids will suffice. If specimens thought to contain high-risk pathogens are processed, or if the machine requires disinfection before servicing, then after flushing with distilled water, the liquid flow channels must be flushed with a strong solution of a chlorine-based agent (2500 p.p.m. available chlorine), provided that no metal components are involved, or 2% glutaraldehyde or an appropriate peroxygen compound for 10 min followed by more distilled water. Before used dialyser membranes are changed the system must first be flushed with distilled water or wash fluid, and then with a strong solution of a chlorine-based agent or peroxygen compound for 10 min, and finally with more distilled water.

In very exceptional circumstances it may be necessary to disinfect the external surfaces of complex automated equipment.

Cryostats in histopathology laboratories

Disinfection is required after sectioning specimens thought to contain high-risk pathogens (category 3) and when defrosting for normal maintenance. Microtomes must be disinfected by soaking the removable parts in 2% glutaraldehyde or 70% ethanol for at least 10 min. The inside of the cabinet must be disinfected with formaldehyde vapour as described previously for exhaust protective cabinets.

Miscellaneous

A wipe impregnated with, for example, 70% ethanol or 60–70% isopropanol can be used to disinfect a physically clean surface, e.g. of electrical equipment, for which immersion or soaking in disinfectant is impractical. The surface must remain wet with alcohol for a minimum of 1 min. The flammability of alcohols must be taken into consideration.

Safe use of glutaraldehyde

Glutaraldehyde may be occasionally required for the disinfection of equipment likely to be damaged by chlorine. Disinfection should, where possible, be carried out in a fume cabinet. If glutaraldehyde must be used in an open laboratory, every effort must be made to avoid exposure of staff to fumes or contact (see occupational exposure standards, pp. 24–25). A chlorine-based agent can be used infrequently on some metals such as good-quality stainless steel, but must be rapidly removed after short exposure and surfaces rinsed thoroughly. Alternatives such as 70% ethanol or peroxygen compounds are another possibility and may be preferable depending on the disinfection requirements and other factors such as corrosion and flammability.

Use of disinfectants in the post-mortem room

(See also Health Services Advisory Committee, 1991b.)

The environment should be thoroughly cleaned and disinfected using a phenolic disinfectant at the concentration required for 'dirty' conditions (see Table 1, p. 8). Walls do not require daily disinfection or cleaning unless obviously contaminated. A solution of a chlorine-based agent should be used if there is a risk of viral infection (especially by HIV and HBV). Chlorine-based agents are corrosive to metals and should be removed rapidly by rinsing. Peroxygen compounds may be a possible alternative.

Instruments should be cleaned and disinfected in a washer–disinfector or autoclaved after thorough cleaning. However, immersion in a phenolic disinfectant for a minimum of 20 min is adequate if an autoclave is unavailable. Glutaraldehyde (not hypochlorite), in a closed container, should be used on instruments after a post-mortem on a patient with a suspected viral infection but heat disinfection is preferable. (See occupational exposure standards, pp. 24–25.)

Hands should be routinely washed thoroughly with soap and water, but if there is a specific infection hazard an antiseptic detergent may be used; an alcohol rub after washing is a convenient method of ensuring adequate disinfection.

References

HEALTH SERVICES ADVISORY COMMITTEE. 1991a. *Safe working and prevention of infection in clinical laboratories.* London: HMSO.

HEALTH SERVICES ADVISORY COMMITTEE. 1991b. *Safe working and prevention of infection in the mortuary and post-mortem room.* London: HMSO.

APPENDIX 1:
SUMMARY OF POLICY FOR DECONTAMINATION OF EQUIPMENT OR ENVIRONMENT

The following summary is reproduced with amendments from Ayliffe GAJ, Lowbury EJL, Geddes AM, Williams JD (eds). 1992. *Control of Hospital Infection: A practical handbook.* 3rd Edn. London: Chapman & Hall.

The following abbreviations have been used in this summary to refer to certain categories of disinfection:

Heat   Autoclave if materials are not likely to be damaged by high temperatures; otherwise use a washer–disinfector, low-temperature steam or pasteurisation

Phen   Clear soluble phenolics at the use-dilution recommended for 'clean' conditions, unless otherwise specified. (See Table 1, p. 8)

Cl   Chlorine-based agents (see Table 2, p. 10, for concentrations)

Glut   2% alkaline-buffered glutaraldehyde (see Table 3, p. 43, for immersion times)

Alc   70% ethanol or industrial methylated spirit (80–90% for non-enveloped viruses); 60–70% isopropanol

Although chlorine-based agents are commonly recommended instead of phenolics for routine disinfection, their frequent use should be avoided because of possible damage to certain materials such as bleaching of fabrics and corrosion of metals.

Thorough rinsing is necessary after use of most chemical disinfectants, especially glutaraldehyde. Alcohol solutions can be allowed to dry without rinsing.

Equipment or site	Routine or preferred method	Acceptable alternative or additional recommendations
Airways and endotracheal tubes	(1) Single use; (2) Heat	(3) Chemical disinfection Cl depending on materials. For patients with tuberculosis use single-use or heat
Baths	*Non-infected patients:* wipe with detergent solution and rinse; cream cleaner may be used for stain and scum removal	*Infected patients and patients with open wounds:* Cl with detergent or non-abrasive powder
Bed-frames	Wash with detergent and dry	After infected patient, Cl or Phen
Bedpans	Washer–disinfector or use single-use and macerator. Wash carriers for single-use pans after use	*Patients with enteric infections:* If 'routine method' not possible, heat disinfection after emptying and washing, or chemical disinfection with Cl
Bowls (surgical)	Autoclave	
Bowls (washing)	Wash and dry, store inverted	For infected patients use individual bowls and disinfect on discharge; (1) Heat disinfection (2) Cl or Phen
Carpets	Vacuum daily; clean periodically by hot water extraction	For known contaminated spills clean with detergent, disinfect with agent that does not damage carpet (see p. 31)
Cheatles forceps	Avoid use	If used, autoclave daily and store in fresh Phen
Crockery and cutlery	(1) Machine wash with rinse temperature above 80°C and air dry; (2) Hand wash by approved method	For patients with enteric infections or open tuberculosis, if possible heat disinfect; if not, use single-use
Drains	Clean regularly	Chemical disinfection is not advised

Equipment or site	Routine or preferred method	Acceptable alternative or additional recommendations
Duvets	Water-impermeable cover: wash with detergent solution and dry	If contaminated disinfect with Phen or Cl (these agents will damage the fabric if used too often)
Endoscopes	See pp. 42–48	
Feeding bottles and teats	Pre-sterilised or terminally heat-treated feeds	Teats and bottles sterilised and packed by SSD. Cl should only be used in small units where other methods are unavailable
Floors (dry cleaning)	(1) Vacuum clean; (2) dust-attracting dry mop	Do not use brooms in patient areas
Floors (wet cleaning)	Wash with detergent solution; disinfection not routinely required	Known contaminated area: Cl or Phen
Furniture and fittings	Damp dust with detergent solution	Known contaminated and special areas, damp dust with Cl or Phen
Infant incubators	Wash with detergent and dry with disposable wipe	*Infected patients*: after cleaning, wipe with Alc or Cl (125 p.p.m. av Cl)
Instruments	Heat	
Locker tops	See furniture and fittings	
Mattresses	Water impermeable cover, wash with detergent solution and dry	Disinfect with Cl or Phen if contaminated; do not disinfect unnecessarily as this damages the mattress cover
Mops (dish)	Do not use	
Mops (dry, dust-attracting)	Do not use for more than two days without reprocessing or washing	Vacuuming after each use may prolong effective life between processing or washing

Equipment or site	Routine or preferred method	Acceptable alternative or additional recommendations
Mops (wet)	Washing machine/dry daily. If not available, rinse after each use, wring and store dry. Heat disinfect periodically	If chemical disinfection is required, rinse in water, soak in Cl (1000 p.p.m. av Cl for 30 min) rinse and store dry
Nail-brushes (surgeons' hands)	Use only if essential	A sterile nail-brush should be used
Pillows	Treat as mattresses	
Razors (safety and open)	Disposable or autoclaved	Alc immersion 10 min
Razors (electric)	Immerse head in Alc 10 min	
Rooms (terminal cleaning or disinfection)	*Non-infected patients:* wash surfaces in detergent solution	*Infected patients:* wash surfaces in 500 p.p.m. av Cl or Phen. Fogging not recommended
Shaving brushes	Do not use for clinical shaving	Autoclave. Use brushless cream or shaving foam
Sputum container	Single-use only	
Thermometers (oral)	(1) Individual thermometers: wipe with Alc, store dry; terminally disinfect as (2). Preferably use single-use sleeve	(2) Collect after round, wipe clean and disinfect with Phen or Alc for 10 min, rinse (if Phen), wipe and store dry
Thermometers (rectal)	Clean with Alc and treat as (2) above	
Thermometers (electronic clinical)	(1) Use single-use sleeve; (2) single-patient use; (3) immerse probe in Alc for 10 min	Do not use without sleeve for oral or rectal temperatures or for patients with an infectious disease
Toilet seats	Wash with detergent and dry	After use by infected patient, or if grossly contaminated, Cl or Phen, rinse and dry

Equipment or site	Routine or preferred method	Acceptable alternative or additional recommendations
Tonometer prisms	Wash, 500 p.p.m. av Cl for 10 min then rinse	
Tooth mugs	(1) Single patient use	(2) If non-disposable, heat disinfection
Toys	Clean first but do not soak soft toys. If contaminated, disinfect by (a) heat, e.g. washing machine, or (b) wiping surface with Alc or Cl	Expensive or treasured toys may withstand low-temperature steam (LTS), gaseous formaldehyde or ethylene oxide; the last mentioned needs long aeration. Heavily contaminated soft toys may have to be destroyed
Trolley tops (dressings)	(1) Clean with detergent and dry at beginning of dressing round only	(2) If contaminated clean first then use Cl, Phen and wipe dry, or Alc
Tubing (anaesthetic or ventilator)	Heat disinfection: (a) washer-disinfector or (b) low-temperature steam	For patients with tuberculosis (1) use single-use tubing (2) Heat (a) or (b)
Urinals	(1) Use washer with *heat* disinfection cycle or use single-use with macerator	(2) Use Cl or Phen. If a tank is used it must be emptied, dried and refilled at least weekly. Avoid disinfectant if possible
Ventilator (mechanical)	See p. 41	
Wash-basins	Clean with detergent. Use cream cleaner for stains, scum, etc. Disinfection not normally required	Disinfection may be required if contaminated. Use Cl detergent solutions or non-abrasive Cl powder
X-ray equipment	Damp dust with detergent solution; switch off; do not over-wet; allow to dry before use	Clean then wipe with Alc to disinfect

APPENDIX 2:
TESTING OF DISINFECTANTS

In most countries, nationally-recognised methods, and other methods, usually exist for testing disinfectants, but those adopted by different professions (e.g. food, medicine and veterinary) vary. The best-known tests for environmental and instrument disinfection are those of the American Association of Official Analytical Chemists (AOAC), the German Society for Hygiene and Microbiology (DGHM), The French standards organisation (AFNOR) and the Dutch Standard Suspension Test (5-5-5). In the UK the improved Kelsey–Sykes capacity test is commonly accepted for environmental disinfectants used in hospitals. A European system of tests is being developed and a suspension test has been agreed by the Council of Europe for use in the food industry (Council of Europe, 1987). It seems likely that this or a similar test will be accepted as a preliminary means of assessing disinfectants for medical use in Europe, but further discussion is required before tests for disinfection of surfaces and other practical tests become accepted. These tests measure different aspects of disinfection and the results of any one test cannot be compared satisfactorily with the results of others.

No nationally-recognised tests for skin disinfection exist in the UK, but those of the Hospital Infection Research Laboratory, in Birmingham, are generally accepted and those of Rotter and colleagues are accepted in some European countries (see Rotter and Ayliffe, 1991). European tests based on these are being developed.

In-use tests

These tests are designed to check not only the performance of a particular disinfectant in use, but also the way in which it is used. They should be performed in the early stages of the implementation of a disinfection policy, and periodically thereafter.

Non-hypochlorite disinfectants

This test (Maurer, 1985) is based on the principle that the main hazard is the possibility of pathogens surviving and multiplying in the disinfectant thus creating a possible source of infection. The suitability of the diluent/inactivator for use in the test must be established by the method described in British Standard BS 6471:1984 before this test is performed. The procedure is as follows:

Using a sterile pipette, transfer 1 mL of disinfectant in use into a sterile container with 9 mL of an appropriate diluent/inactivator, e.g. 3% Tween 80. Within 1 h, transfer 0.2 mL of the mixed disinfectant–diluent/inactivator on to the surface of each of two well-dried nutrient agar plates. Incubate one plate at 32°C or 37°C for three days, and the other at room temperature for seven days, and examine for bacterial colonies. The disinfectant sample is deemed to have failed the test if five or more colonies grow on either plate (equivalent to 250 or more viable bacteria per millilitre of the disinfectant sample).

Reasons for failure include the following:
• Incorrect measurement of the disinfectant or water when preparing the use-dilution
• Diluted disinfectant kept in use for too long
• Reuse of containers that have not been washed and heat-disinfected
• 'Topping up' a container in which the diluted disinfectant has been partly used
• The presence of an inactivating material
• An inappropriate choice of disinfectant
• The presence of bacterial spores in the diluted disinfectant.

Hypochlorite

The presence of available chlorine in hypochlorite solutions can be checked rapidly with starch–iodide indicator paper, which changes colour to dark blue-black if the solution is of adequate strength (200 p.p.m. or above). When in contact with solutions that are either under strength (100 p.p.m. or below) or totally exhausted, the indicator colour varies from pale-blue to white. Strong hypochlorite solutions may bleach colour development rapidly such that the paper appears to remain white. If a blue-black colour fails to appear, test a 1% (approximately) dilution of the hypochlorite; if a colour still fails to develop, the solution has negligible available chlorine. It is best to check solutions after disinfection should have occurred, immediately prior to discard.

Chlorine assay

Hypochlorite solutions tend to decompose on storage and progressively lose available chlorine. The level of available chlorine present in a solution at a particular time can be determined by the following method:

Titrate a 5 mL sample with 0.141M sodium arsenite solution, stirring with a thin glass rod. The end point occurs when a drop of the mixture, withdrawn on the rod, does not produce a purple/black coloration on starch–iodide paper. The titration in millilitres gives the available chlorine content directly in grams per litre ($1\% = 10\,g\,L^{-1} = 10\,000$ p.p.m.).

Appropriate dilution of either the hypochlorite or arsenite solution makes possible assay of any concentration of available chlorine at 10 p.p.m. or above.

Use-dilution tests

The function of a use-dilution test (e.g. the Kelsey-Sykes capacity test, Kelsey and Maurer 1974) is to indicate a practical working concentration, i.e. the dilution to be made in water, of a particular disinfectant for a particular purpose, e.g. for disinfecting floors or decontaminating items in laboratory discard jars. Use-dilution tests must reflect actual conditions of use of the disinfectant, and are usually neither quick nor easy to perform. Hence the testing of a new product leading to suggested use-dilutions should be left to specialist, independent laboratories with the necessary expertise. The principle of the Kelsey-Sykes test should be understood by those responsible for producing a disinfection policy. The test, which is most suitable for phenolic disinfectants, suggests one use-dilution for 'clean' conditions, and another for 'dirty' conditions. The test for dirty conditions includes the addition of yeast and is appropriate for use of disinfectants in the presence of organic matter, e.g. blood or pus. The use-dilutions derived serve well as preliminary trial dilutions that can be modified by experience gained by in-use testing.

References

MAURER IM. 1985. *Hospital hygiene*. 3rd edn. Bristol: Wright PSG.

COUNCIL OF EUROPE. 1987. *Test methods for the antimicrobial activity of disinfectants in food hygiene*. Strasbourg: Council of Europe.

KELSEY JC, MAURER IM. 1974. An improved (1974) Kelsey-Sykes test for disinfectants. *Pharm J*, **207**, 528-30.

ROTTER ML, AYLIFFE GAJ. 1991. *Practical guide on rationale and testing procedure for disinfection of hands*. World Health Organisation.

SELECTED BIBLIOGRAPHY

General

AYLIFFE GAJ, COLLINS BJ, TAYLOR LJ. 1990. *Hospital-acquired infection: principles and prevention.* 2nd edn. London: Wright.

AYLIFFE GAJ, LOWBURY EJL, GEDDES AM, WILLIAMS JD. 1992. *Control of hospital infection: a practical handbook.* 3rd edn. London: Chapman & Hall.

BENNETT J, BRACHMAN PS (EDS). 1992. *Hospital infections.* 3rd edn. Boston: Little Brown and Co.

BLOCK SS (ED). 1991. *Disinfection, sterilisation and preservation.* 3rd edn. Philadelphia: Lea and Febiger.

COLLINS CH. 1988. *Laboratory-acquired infection.* 2nd edn. London: Butterworth.

GARDNER JF, PEEL MM. 1991. *Introduction to sterilization, disinfection and infection control.* 2nd edn. Edinburgh: Churchill Livingstone.

MAURER IM. 1985. *Hospital hygiene.* 3rd edn. Bristol: Wright PSG.

RUSSELL AD, HUGO WB, AYLIFFE GAJ, (EDS). 1992. *Principles and practice of disinfection, preservation and sterilization.* 2nd edn. Oxford: Blackwell Scientific.

WENZEL RP (ED). 1993. *Prevention and control of nosocomial infections.* 2nd edn. Baltimore: Williams and Wilkins.

Guidelines

ADVISORY COMMITTEE ON DANGEROUS PATHOGENS. 1990. *HIV – the causative agent of AIDS and related conditions.* 2nd revision of guidelines. London: HMSO.

BRITISH MEDICAL ASSOCIATION. 1989. *A code of practice for sterilization of instruments and control of cross-infection.* London: BMA.

BRITISH SOCIETY OF GASTROENTEROLOGY. 1988. Cleaning and disinfection of equipment for gastrointestinal flexible endoscopy: interim recommendations of a working party of the British Society of Gastroenterology. *Gut,* **29**, 1134-51.

BRITISH THORACIC SOCIETY. 1989. Bronchoscopy and infection control. *Lancet*, **2**, 270-1.

CENTRAL STERILISING CLUB. 1986. *Working Party Report No.2: sterilisation and disinfection of heat-labile equipment.* (Obtainable from the Hospital Infection Research Laboratory, Dudley Road Hospital, Birmingham B18 7QH.)

COOKE RP, FENELEY RC, AYLIFFE G, LAWRENCE WT, EMMERSON AM, GREENGRASS SM. 1993. Decontamination of urological equipment: interim report of a working group. *Brit J Urol*, **71**, 5-9.

DEPARTMENT OF HEALTH AND SOCIAL SECURITY. 1977. *Memorandum on rabies.* London: HMSO.

DEPARTMENT OF HEALTH AND SOCIAL SECURITY. 1986. *Memorandum on the control of viral haemorrhagic fevers.* London: HMSO.

DEPARTMENT OF HEALTH AND SOCIAL SECURITY. 1987. *Health Service Catering Manual: Hygiene.* London: HMSO.

DEPARTMENT OF HEALTH AND SOCIAL SECURITY. 1987. *Hospital laundry arrangements for used and infected linen.* London: HMSO.

DEPARTMENT OF HEALTH AND SOCIAL SECURITY. 1989. *Report of the Expert Advisory Committee on Biocides.* London: HMSO.

DEPARTMENT OF HEALTH AND SOCIAL SECURITY. 1989. *Health Service guidelines in precooked chilled food.* London: HMSO.

DEPARTMENT OF HEALTH AND SOCIAL SECURITY. 1990. *Guidance for clinical health care workers. Protection against infection with HIV and hepatitis viruses. Recommendations of the Expert Advisory Group in AIDS.* London: HMSO.

DEPARTMENT OF HEALTH AND SOCIAL SECURITY. 1990. *Report of the Group of Experts. Cryptosporidium in water supplies.* London: HMSO.

HEALTH AND SAFETY EXECUTIVE. Control of Substances Hazardous to Health Regulations (1988). London: HMSO.

HEALTH SERVICES ADVISORY COMMITTEE. 1981. *The safe disposal of clinical waste.* London: HMSO.

HEALTH SERVICES ADVISORY COMMITTEE. 1991:
- *Safe working and prevention of infection in clinical laboratories*
- *Safe working and prevention of infection in clinical laboratories – model rules for staff and visitors*
- *Safe working and prevention of infection in the mortuary and post-mortem room.* London: HMSO.

HOFFMAN PN, COOKE EM, LARKIN DP, ET AL. 1988. Control of infection in general practice: a survey and recommendations. *BMJ*, **297**, 34-6.

COMBINED WORKING PARTY OF THE HOSPITAL INFECTION SOCIETY AND THE BRITISH SOCIETY OF ANTIMICROBIAL CHEMOTHERAPY. 1990. Revised guidelines for the control of epidemic methicillin-resistant *Staphylococcus aureus*. *J Hosp Infect*, **16**, 351-77.

RUTALA WA. 1990. APIC guidelines for the selection and use of disinfectants. *Am J Infect Control*, **18**, 99-117.

SPELLER DCE, SHANSON DC, AYLIFFE GAJ, COOKE EM. 1990. Acquired immune deficiency syndrome: recommendations of a Working Party of the Hospital Infection Society. *J Hosp Infect*, **15**, 7-34.

Standards

BRITISH STANDARDS INSTITUTION. 1984. *BS 6471: Determination of antimicrobial value of QAC disinfectant formulations*. London: British Standards Institution.

COUNCIL OF EUROPE. 1987. *Test methods for the antibacterial activity of disinfectants*. Strasbourg: Council of Europe.

KELSEY JC, MAURER IM. 1974. An improved Kelsey–Sykes test for disinfectants. *Pharm J*, **213**, 528-30.

ROTTER ML, AYLIFFE GAJ. 1991. *Practical guide on rationale and testing procedure for disinfection of hands*. World Health Organisation.

Acknowledgement

The authors wish to thank JR Babb and CR Bradley for their advice on endoscope disinfection.